Contents

Key

* easy
** medium
*** difficult

German food

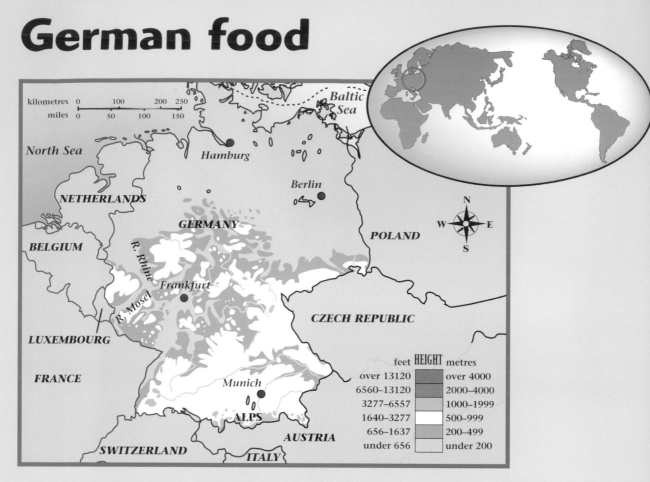

Germany is in the centre of Europe. The land is very varied, with sandy beaches in the north and the snowy peaks of the Alps to the south.

Around the country

The area around the north and east is low and flat. It can be cold and damp here, so people like to cook warming food, such as soup and roasted meat (often served with fruit). Pickled meats and herrings are also popular. People in this region like to add lemon juice or vinegar to their food for a sour taste.

The centre of Germany has forests and **fertile** river valleys. Hams from **wild boar** and pigs are specialities, as well as Bratwurst (sausage), sauerkraut (cabbage **fermented** with salt) and potato dumplings. Vineyards and orchards produce grapes, apples and pears. **Rye**, a grain used for making bread, is also grown here.

4

▶ *Many German towns have open air markets selling a wide variety of fresh food.*

In the south it is more hilly. Cows graze here, and **vines** grow along the Mosel and Rhine river valleys. Farmers grow barley for brewing beer and wheat for making bread.

In the past

For hundreds of years, Germany was made up of small kingdoms ruled by princes who enjoyed hunting, and then roasting the meat on open fires. Feasts often lasted as long as eight hours! Today, Germany is a federation, which means it is made up of many states (called *Länder*). Each state is different, so Germany has many styles of cooking and special regional dishes.

German meals

Germans enjoy simple, hearty meals. Breakfast (*Frühstück*) consists of a choice of breads, jam and cold meats. Cheeses, boiled eggs, yoghurt, fruit juice and small pastries may also be served, especially at the weekend. Lunch (*Mittagessen*) is usually the main meal of the day and often includes dumplings, noodles or potatoes with meat. Dessert might be jelly and fruit, or a slice of gâteau (cake).

The evening meal (*Abendessen*) may consist of a cold meal of open sandwiches or a cold meat platter, with gherkins, radishes and tomatoes. Germans also enjoy a number of festivals during the year in which food, wine and beer play an important part.

5

Ingredients

cabbages

breads

beetroot

radishes

sausages

sauerkraut

ham

gherkins

cheese

apples

mushrooms

morello cherries

pears

sausages

Bread

German bread is often made with **rye** flour, which has a rich, nutty taste. German bakeries have a very wide range of bread and rolls. Outside Germany you can buy German breads from larger supermarkets.

Dill

Dill is a feathery-leafed herb with a slight aniseed flavour, a bit like liquorice.

Fruit

Apples and pears are plentiful in Germany and are often made into juice. Apple or pear juice is a favourite German drink.

Ham

Ham is made from pork legs. German hams are cured, which means they are soaked in very salty water. They are also smoked by hanging the hams over a smoky fire. Burning different woods in the fire gives the hams different flavours.

Morello cherries

Morello cherries have a slightly sour taste. You can buy them in jars or cans in a sugar syrup.

Pickles

Any vegetable or fruit which is preserved in jars of vinegar is called a pickle. Gherkins are small pickled cucumbers. They are sold in jars, and sometimes flavoured with dill and white peppercorns. Pickled beetroot is a favourite food, too.

Sauerkraut

Sauerkraut is white cabbage that is layered with salt and allowed to **ferment**. It has a sharp, tangy taste. You can buy it in large jars in supermarkets. Germans eat it with hot or cold meats.

Sausages

Sausages are very popular in Germany. Here are some that you may find at your local supermarket or delicatessen: Bratwurst – pork or veal sausages that need to be fried or grilled; Schinkenwurst – ham sausage; Bockwurst – a type of hot dog sausage; Bierwurst – pork and beef sausage which is cut into thick slices and grilled; Extrawurst – cooked sausage that is eaten cold in slices.

Cheese

The most popular cheese is called Speisequark, or quark. It is ideal as a dip, spread on bread, or baked in a cheesecake (see page 34). Buy it in tubs from the chiller cabinet of larger supermarkets. Another favourite is Tilsut, a creamy yellow cheese with little holes running through it. People in Germany often serve a selection of cheeses with a cold meat platter as a supper dish, with bread and pickles.

Before you start

Kitchen rules

There are a few basic rules you should always follow when you are cooking:

- Ask an adult if you can use the kitchen.
- Some cooking processes, especially those involving hot water or oil, can be dangerous. When you see this sign, take extra care and ask an adult for help.
- Wash your hands before you start.
- Wear an apron to protect your clothes, and tie back long hair.
- Be very careful when you use sharp knives.
- Never leave pan handles sticking out in case you knock them.
- Always wear oven gloves to lift things in and out of the oven.
- Wash fruits and vegetables before you use them.
- Always wash chopping boards very well after use.

How long will it take?

Some of the recipes in this book are quick and easy, and some are more difficult and take longer. The strip across the top of the right hand page of each recipe tells you how long it will take you to cook each dish from start to finish. It also shows how difficult each dish is to make: every recipe is
* (easy), ** (medium) or *** (difficult).

Quantities and measurements

You can see how many people each recipe will serve at the top of each right hand page. You can multiply or divide the quantities if you want to cook for more or fewer people.

Ingredients for recipes can be measured in two ways. Metric measurements use grams and millilitres. Imperial measurements use ounces and fluid ounces. This book uses metric measurements. If you want to convert these into imperial measurements, see the chart on page 44.

In the recipes you will see the following abbreviations:

tbsp = tablespoon   g = grams   cm = centimetre
tsp = teaspoon   ml = millilitres

Utensils

To cook the recipes in this book, you will need these utensils (as well as kitchen essentials, such as spoons, plates and bowls):

- chopping board
- food processor or blender
- 18cm heavy based non-stick frying pan
- flameproof casserole dish
- rolling pin
- electric whisk
- sieve
- small and large saucepans with lid
- measuring spoons
- set of scales
- sharp knife
- baking sheets
- 2 x 20cm round cake tins
- 23cm loose-bottomed flan tin
- icing **piping** set
- ladle
- 900g loaf tin
- grater
- colander

 Whenever you use kitchen knives, be very careful.

Pancake soup

Winter can be very cold in Germany. Cooks make this warming soup more filling by adding slices of pancake to it. Make the pancakes first, and add them before serving the soup.

What you need

50g plain flour
1 egg
125ml milk
2 tsp of vegetable oil
  (or small knob of **lard**)
2 beef, chicken or vegetable
  stock cubes
2 tbsp fresh chopped chives
  or parsley, to **garnish**

What you do

1 Sift the flour into a bowl.

2 Lightly **beat** the egg and milk together.

3 Make a well in the centre of the flour and stir in half the egg mixture. Beat well.

4 Gradually beat in the rest of the milk and egg to make a pancake batter.

(!) 5 Put some of the oil or lard into an 18cm non-stick frying pan. Heat gently. Tilt the pan to spread the lard or oil. Add 1–2 tbsp of pancake batter and tilt the pan, so that it spreads out thinly.

6 Cook gently for 2–3 minutes until the mixture has set and is golden brown underneath. Using a fish slice or spatula, turn the pancake. Cook until it is lightly browned. Slide it onto a plate. Make 6 pancakes.

7 Roll up each pancake and cut it into 1cm wide strips.

8 Put 800ml of water into a saucepan. Crumble in the stock cubes and heat until **simmering**. Add the pancake strips and heat for 1 minute.

9 Ladle into soup bowls. Scatter chives or parsley over each bowl and serve hot.

Rye bread

German breads are quite firm, so they are ideal for open sandwiches, which are very popular in Germany. To make them, butter slices of bread and add sausage, cheese, hard-boiled egg, herring fillets or pickles.

What you need

350g **rye** flour
350g strong
   wholemeal flour
½ tsp salt
7g sachet easy-blend
   yeast
3 tbsp vegetable oil
   or 40g **lard**
3 tbsp honey
200ml hand-warm water
100ml hand-warm milk
a little oil for brushing

What you do

1 Put the flours, salt and yeast into a bowl or food processor. Add the oil or lard and honey and add enough water and milk to make a soft but not sticky dough. (If using a food processor, slowly add the liquid through the funnel until the dough forms a ball.)

2 **Knead** the dough – 10 minutes by hand or 3 minutes by processor (see page 13).

3 Put the dough in a bowl. Brush a little oil over some cling film. **Cover** the bowl with the cling film (oil side down) and leave in a warm place for about 1 hour or until the dough has doubled in size.

4 Knead the dough again – 5 minutes by hand or 2–3 minutes in a processor.

5 Mould the dough into a brick shape and put it into a 900g loaf tin. Press the dough into the corners. Cover with oiled cling film and leave in a warm place for 40 minutes, or until the dough has risen.

6 Preheat the oven to 210°C/425°F/gas mark 7.

7 Bake the loaf for 25–30 minutes, or until the bread sounds hollow when you tap it.

8 Cool the bread for 10 minutes, then turn it out onto a wire rack to cool before serving.

KNEADING DOUGH

Put the dough on a floured surface and stretch it out with one hand. Then fold the dough back in half and press down with your palm. Turn it a little and pull and fold again until the dough feels elastic. You can also use a food processor to knead dough.

USEFUL YEAST

Yeast is a living thing. If it is made warm and damp and given sugar for food, it grows and makes bubbles. The bubbles make foods like bread rise. High temperatures kill the yeast, so any liquid added to it must only be warm, not hot.

Cold meat platter

Meat platters are very popular in Germany. People often serve them for the evening meal, or for a special breakfast.

What you need

4 eggs

250g selection of cold meats (e.g. Bierwurst, Extrawurst, Salami, Cervelat or Westphalian ham)

8 slices of German bread or rolls or some of each

8 gherkins

What you do

1 Put the eggs in a saucepan. **Cover** with water, bring to the boil and **simmer** for 10 minutes.

2 Meanwhile, arrange the cold meats on a large plate. Start with the larger slices, then add the smaller slices, rolling or folding some of them.

3 Lift the eggs out of the pan. Put them in a bowl of cold water and tap the shells to crack them.

4 When the eggs are cold, **peel** off the shells. Cut them into halves, quarters or slice them. Arrange them around the meats.

5 **Slice** each gherkin lengthways, without cutting all the way to the end. Spread the slices out into a 'fan'.

6 Arrange the gherkins on the platter. Serve with a selection of German breads, butter and extra pickles.

GERMAN MEATS

There are around 80 types of meat, sausage and ham in Germany. Sausages range from spicy to mild in flavour, and from smooth to coarse, with large chunks of meat, in texture. For a platter, try to choose a good variety of meats.

GERMAN BREADS

German breads are often made with **rye**. There are over 200 different varieties. Look out for Vollkornbrot (whole wheat bread), which goes well with cheese and ham. Landbrot is Germany's everyday bread and is made with rye and wheat flours. Pumpernickel is a strongly-flavoured dark rye bread.

15

Herrings in soured cream

Germans eat herrings smoked, pickled, sprinkled with a flavoured oil or added to salads. This recipe is for herrings in an onion and sour cream **marinade**. It was a favourite of the German leader Prince von Bismarck in the late 1800s, and is still called Bismarck Herring.

What you need

4 roll mop herrings
   (pickled herrings in vinegar)
2 tbsp lemon juice
142ml pot soured cream
75ml natural yoghurt
1 onion
1 eating apple
1 tsp fresh chopped dill
sprigs of dill to **garnish**

What you do

1 Put a sieve over a bowl. Place the herrings in the sieve and leave them to **drain**.

2 Stir the lemon juice, soured cream and yoghurt together.

3 **Peel** the onion and **slice** it into thin rings.

4 Slice the apple into quarters. Cut out the core. Cut three of the pieces into small cubes.

5 Stir the onion, diced apple and chopped dill into the soured cream mixture. Gently toss the herrings in the mixture to coat them.

6 Put the roll mops on a serving dish and spoon the sauce around them. Slice the remaining piece of apple and use it with the sprigs of dill to garnish the herrings.

SOURED CREAM

Soured cream that you buy in shops has been made by adding a special ingredient to single cream to make it go sour. You should not use cream that has simply gone off. To make your own soured cream, stir in 1 tsp lemon juice to 142ml single cream and leave for 30 minutes, to allow the cream to thicken.

17

Pork and apple casserole

This warming dish from northern Germany is ideal for a winter's day. The long, slow method of cooking makes the pork very tender. The apple thickens the stock to make a tangy sauce. You will need to use a casserole dish that you can also use on the hob.

What you need

2 onions
1 tbsp vegetable oil or 25g **lard**
4 thick pork chops
1 pork or vegetable stock cube
2 tsp dried mixed herbs
1 tsp caraway seeds
100g button mushrooms
1 large cooking apple

What you do

1 **Preheat** the oven to 180°C/350°F/gas mark 4.

2 **Peel** the onions and **slice** them thinly.

(!) 3 Heat the oil or lard in a casserole dish. **Fry** the onions for 2 minutes.

4 Add the pork chops and cook for 3 minutes, or until browned on one side. Turn them over to brown the other side.

5 Crumble the stock cube in 600ml of hot water and stir until it **dissolves**. Add the dried herbs, caraway seeds and stock to the casserole. Bring to the **boil** and **cover**.

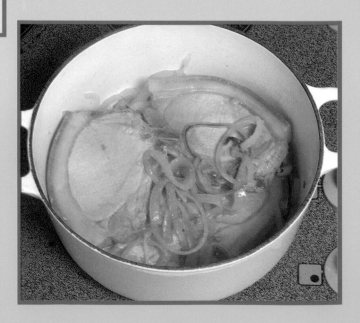

6 Wearing oven gloves, carefully put the casserole into the oven to cook.

7 After 1½ hours of cooking time, wash the mushrooms. Peel the apple and take out the core. Roughly chop it.

8 Add the mushrooms and apple to the casserole. Make sure they are covered with stock. Add extra hot water if necessary.

9 **Cover** and cook for a further 25 minutes, or until the apple is very soft and the mushrooms are tender.

10 Serve hot with boiled potatoes or potato dumplings (see page 26).

Pork and beef rissoles

German cooks often use beef and pork mince in the same recipe to give a richer flavour. Beef rissoles have become known as beefburgers, which are often called by their American name – hamburgers.

What you need

125g pork mince
125g beef mince
1 thick slice stale bread, crusts removed
1 small onion
1 small egg
1 tbsp oil
2 tomatoes to **garnish**

What you do

1 Mix the pork and beef mince together with a fork.

2 Cut the bread into quarters. Put into a blender or food processor and process to make breadcrumbs.

3 **Peel** the onion. **Slice** off a few rings and set aside. Finely **chop** the rest.

4 Lightly **beat** the egg. Mix together the meat, bread, onion, egg and salt and pepper.

5 Put a 16cm crumpet ring onto a lightly floured surface. Put half the meat mixture into the ring and press down well with the back of a spoon.

6 Lift the ring off. Repeat this to make the second rissole. You can also shape the rissoles with lightly floured hands. Press the mixture together well to prevent it coming apart during cooking.

(!) **7** Heat the oil in a frying pan. Cook the rissoles over a medium heat for 5 minutes on each side. You can **grill** the rissoles rather than **fry** them if you like.

8 **Garnish** with sliced tomato and the onion rings. Serve hot with some sauerkraut or pickles.

FAST FOOD, GERMAN STYLE

The Americans have made the hamburger a world-famous fast food. The Germans have their own fast food. You can buy frankfurter sausages served with curry sauce from take-away stands on the street.

21

Vienna-style escalopes

This recipe did not come from Vienna (or Wien in German)– the capital of Austria. This style of cooking pork or veal actually came from Italian cooks, who had borrowed the idea from the Spanish! It is a very popular dish in Germany, where it is called Wiener Schnitzel. Choose pork or veal **escalopes**, boned loin chops or pork fillet escalopes for this dish.

What you need

6 slices of one-day-old white bread

4 x 75g pieces of pork or veal

2 tbsp lemon juice

1 egg

25g butter

2 tbsp vegetable oil

1 lemon to **garnish**

What you do

1 Put the bread on baking trays.

2 **Preheat** the oven to 180°C/350°F/gas mark 4. **Bake** the bread for 10–15 minutes until crispy. Leave to cool.

3 Put the bread into a large bowl. Crush it with the end of a rolling pin. Tip the breadcrumbs onto a plate.

4 Put a piece of meat between two pieces of cling film. On a wooden board, hit the meat with a rolling pin to flatten it to about 8mm thick. **Peel** off the cling film. Use scissors to snip around the edge of the meat to stop it curling as it cooks. Repeat for each piece of meat.

5 Put the meat and lemon juice into a small plastic bag. Shake well.

6 Lightly **beat** the egg and pour it onto a plate. Dip each piece of meat into the egg. Let the excess egg drip off and then dip into the breadcrumbs.

(!) 7 Heat the butter and oil in a large frying pan. **Fry** the pieces for 4–5 minutes on each side, or until the meat is cooked through. To test it is cooked, make a small cut in the meat – it should not be pink.

8 Garnish with lemon slices. You could serve the escalopes with boiled potatoes and green beans.

Potato cakes with stewed fruit

In Germany, cooks often serve fruit with **savoury** main course dishes. It is cooked with very little sugar, so that it keeps its sharp taste.

What you need

450g potatoes
½ an onion
1 egg
1 tbsp plain flour
4 tbsp vegetable oil

What you do

1 **Peel** the potatoes and **grate** them.

2 Peel the onion and grate it.

3 Lightly **beat** the egg. Mix together the raw potatoes, onions, flour and egg. Add salt and pepper, and stir well.

(!) 4 Heat the oil in a heavy-based non-stick frying pan. Add tablespoonfuls of the mixture to the frying pan about 5cm apart. (You may have to cook them in batches.) Flatten the potato cakes with a fork and **fry** for 3–4 minutes on each side, or until golden.

5 Serve with stewed apple (see page 42) or stewed cranberries (see page 23 opposite).

Stewed cranberries

You can buy fresh cranberries from the fruit and vegetable counter during December. Frozen cranberries are for sale all year round from the freezer cabinet of larger supermarkets.

What you do

1 Put 175g cranberries and 4 tbsp orange juice into a small saucepan. **Cover** and cook over a low heat for 10 minutes.

2 Stir from time to time, to squash the fruit. Add 4 tbsp sugar and stir until it has dissolved. Taste the fruit, adding a little more sugar if you wish.

3 Cool slightly, and serve with potato cakes.

Cabbage rolls

Cabbage has been a **staple** food for Germans for hundreds of years. It is a vegetable that grows well in Germany, even in the north where it is cold. For this recipe choose a large cabbage and use the larger leaves – throw away the really tough outer leaves first.

What you need

1 medium potato
pinch of salt
1 small onion
100g minced beef
100g minced pork
1 slice bread,
    crusts removed
1 tbsp fresh chopped
    parsley or 1 tsp
    dried parsley
pinch grated nutmeg
1 egg, **beaten**
8 large cabbage leaves
2 rashers smoked
    streaky bacon
1 tbsp oil
1 beef stock cube

What you do

1 Scrub the potato. Cook it in **boiling** water with a pinch of salt for 20 minutes. **Drain** and leave it to cool.

2 **Peel** the onion and finely **chop** it. Put into a bowl with the meat.

3 Cut the bread into quarters and process it in a blender or food processor to make crumbs.

4 Add the breadcrumbs to the minced meat. Mix in the parsley, nutmeg, beaten egg, and salt and pepper.

5 **Peel** and mash the potato. Add it to the mixture.

6 Lay the cabbage leaves in a colander. Put the colander inside a heatproof bowl and place it in the sink.

7 **Cover** the leaves with boiling water from a kettle. Leave for 2 minutes. Lift the colander onto the draining board to drain the cabbage leaves.

8 Spread a leaf out on a wooden board. Spoon meat filling onto the leaf and roll it up, tucking in the sides. Poke in a cocktail stick to fasten it.

9 Repeat step 8 for each leaf.

(!) 10 Chop the bacon. Heat the oil in a flameproof casserole dish or a large saucepan and **fry** the bacon for 2 minutes. Add the cabbage rolls and fry until they are light brown all over.

11 Add enough hot water to cover the rolls. Crumble in the stock cube and bring to the boil. Cover and **simmer** for 25 minutes.

12 Lift the cabbage rolls onto a plate and spoon over the gravy. Serve hot with potatoes or potato dumplings.

27

Potato dumplings

Potato dumplings are popular in Germany. You can either make them with cooked and mashed potato, or with half mashed potato and half raw **grated** potato (as in this recipe). Use a floury variety of potato, such as King Edward.

What you need

900g potatoes
pinch of salt
1 slice of one-day-old
   bread
3 tbsp oil
1 egg
50g plain flour
1 tsp fresh chopped
   parsley

What you do

1 Scrub half the potatoes. Cook them whole for 20 minutes in **boiling** water with a pinch of salt. **Drain** them and leave them to cool.

(!) 2 To make croûtons (cubes of fried bread), cut the bread into ½cm cubes. Heat the oil in a heavy-based saucepan and gently **fry** the cubes until golden. Leave to cool on a plate lined with kitchen towel.

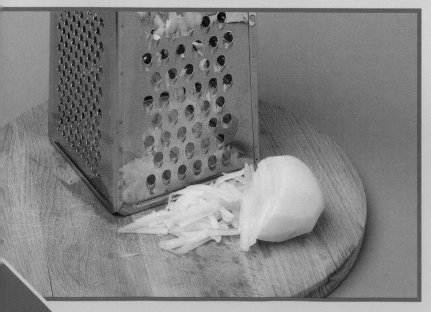

3 **Peel** and mash the cooked potatoes. Peel and finely grate the raw potatoes. Mix the cooked, mashed and grated raw potato together. **Beat** in the egg, flour and a pinch of salt.

4 Put 2 tbsp of the potato mixture in your hand. Press three croûtons in the middle of the mixture.

5 Squash the mixture together and roll into a ball. Repeat this to make 16 dumplings.

6 Bring a large pan of water to the boil. Add the dumplings and bring to the boil again. Lower the heat and **simmer** for 10–15 minutes or until the dumplings float to the surface.

7 Lift the dumplings onto a dish and sprinkle with parsley. Serve hot with cooked meats and a little stewed fruit or sauerkraut.

Braised red cabbage

In the winter months, Germans bake red cabbage to make this warming dish. You can eat it as part of a hot main course with roasted meats and potatoes.

What you need

1 onion
1 red cabbage
2 red apples
2 tbsp vegetable oil
4 tbsp white wine vinegar
3 tbsp brown sugar

What you do

1 **Peel** and finely **slice** the onion.

(!) 2 Throw away the outside leaves of the cabbage. With a sharp knife, cut the cabbage into quarters through the stalk. Cut out and throw away the stalk. Cut the leaves very finely to **shred** the cabbage.

3 **Preheat** the oven to 180°C/350°F/gas mark 4. **Peel** the apples, take out their cores and grate the apple that is left.

(!) 4 Heat the oil in a deep flameproof casserole dish. **Fry** the onion for 2 minutes. Add the cabbage and cook for 4–5 minutes stirring all the time.

5 Stir in the apple, 6 tbsps of water, the vinegar and the sugar. **Cover** tightly and put into the oven. Cook for 1½–2 hours.

6 Stir well and serve hot with potato dumplings (see page 26) or cooked meats.

Red cabbage and bacon salad

In Germany, salads of **grated** or sliced vegetables are often served before the main course with a little sugar and vinegar or lemon juice. This recipe makes enough for 2 people. Replace the bacon with a cooked, finely sliced frankfurter sausage if you prefer.

What you do

1 Finely **slice** 125g red cabbage leaves. Grate 2 carrots and peel and slice 1 small onion.

2 Stir the vegetables together. Sprinkle over 1 tsp caraway seeds, 1 tsp caster sugar and 2 tsp vinegar.

3 **Grill** 2 back rashers of smoked bacon until crispy. When cool, cut off the rind and fat. Finely chop the bacon that is left. Stir the pieces of bacon into the salad and serve.

Potato salad

Germans often cook potatoes before peeling them. This keeps more **nutrients** in the potato. For this salad, you could leave the skin on and just **slice** the potatoes if you prefer. In Germany, people sprinkle their salads with vinegar, lemon juice and a little sugar to give a slightly sour, but refreshing taste.

What you need

900g small potatoes
pinch of salt
2 eggs
4 rashers smoked back
    bacon, (optional)
1 onion
2 sweet and sour gherkins
1 tbsp **capers** (optional)
1 beef stock cube
2 tbsp white wine vinegar
lettuce leaves to **garnish**
    (optional)

What you do

1 Scrub the potatoes. Cook them whole in their skins in a pan of **boiling** water with a pinch of salt for 20 minutes. **Drain** and leave to cool.

2 While the potatoes are cooking, put the eggs in a saucepan. **Cover** them with water and bring to the boil. Turn down the heat and **simmer** for 8 minutes.

3 Lift the eggs out and place in cold water. Tap the shells to crack them. Leave to cool.

4 Using scissors, cut off the bacon rind. **Grill** the bacon until crispy.

5 **Peel** and **chop** the onion.

6 Chop the gherkins, capers and bacon. Peel the eggs and chop them.

7 Peel and **slice** the potatoes. Stir the potatoes, onion, gherkins, capers, bacon and egg together.

8 Pinch off a small piece from the stock cube and **dissolve** it in 4 tbsps of hot water. Mix it with the vinegar and pour it over the potatoes. Serve the salad with the lettuce leaves arranged around it if you wish.

VARIATIONS

For a more meaty salad, add sliced frankfurter sausage to the potatoes. For a **vegetarian** version, leave out the bacon and use vegetable stock instead of meat stock.

Stewed apple

German farmers grow a lot of apples and pears. Some are used to make fruit juice. A favourite drink in Germany is fruit juice mixed with lemonade. Stewed apples are used in both **savoury** and sweet dishes. This dish goes well with potato cakes (page 22). It is called *Apfelmus*.

What you need

1kg cooking apples
3 tbsp sugar

What you do

1 **Slice** the apple away from the core into four or more pieces. Remove the **peel**.

2 Rinse the apple pieces and put them into a heavy-based non-stick saucepan. **Cover** tightly and cook over a very low heat for 5 minutes, stirring now and then. (If you cook the apple too quickly, it will burn on the bottom of the pan.) Cook until the apple has softened.

3 Take the pan off the heat and stir in the sugar. Leave to cool. Add a little more sugar if you want to serve it with muesli or pancakes.

To cook in the microwave

Put the prepared apple in a microwave-proof bowl. Cover with a lid or plate and cook on high for 2 minutes. Stir and cook for 30 seconds more, or until the apple has softened. Stir in the sugar.

Keeping apples

Whole apples don't freeze well, but stewed apples do. If you have an apple tree in your garden, stew the apples and then freeze to enjoy later.

Stew the apples as shown on page 42 and cool completely. Spoon into freezer bags and seal, leaving a bit of space at the top for the mixture to **expand** into as it freezes. Label the bags and store for up to 6 months. When you want to use a bag of stewed apple, **defrost** it overnight in the fridge.

Baked cheesecake

Quark is the most popular cheese in Germany. It is often served spread on bread and sprinkled with a little sugar. Quark is similar to cream cheese.

What you need

300g ready-made
   shortcrust pastry
plain flour for dusting
1 lemon
500g quark
6 tbsp clear honey
1 tbsp cornflour
50g raisins
2 eggs
1 tsp icing sugar

What you do

1 **Preheat** the oven to 200°C/ 400°F/gas mark 6. Put a baking sheet in to heat.

2 Dust a work surface and rolling pin with flour. Roll the rolling pin over the pastry. Turn the pastry a little and roll it again in another direction. Do this until it forms a round shape about 30cm wide.

3 Carefully lay the pastry in a 23cm round loose-bottomed flan tin. Trim off any pastry that is hanging over the edge by rolling the rolling pin over the flat tin.

4 Prick the bottom of the pastry case with a fork and **chill** for 10 minutes.

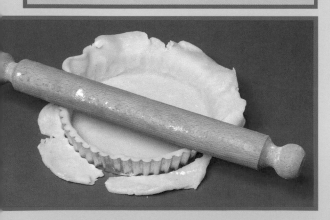

(!) 5 Place strips of foil around the pastry edges to stop the sides from falling in during cooking. Put the tin on the hot baking sheet and bake for 10 minutes.

6 **Grate** the lemon rind finely. In a bowl, mix the quark, honey, cornflour, raisins and lemon rind.

7 Carefully crack open an egg. Keep the yolk in one half of the shell and let the white drip into a bowl. Put the yolk into the quark mixture. Do this with the second egg, too.

8 Using an electric whisk, beat the egg whites until firm and then tip them into the quark mixture. Use a metal spoon to **fold** the whites in, making cutting movements rather than stirring.

9 Spoon the quark mixture into the baked pastry case. Turn the oven to 180°C/350°F/gas mark 4 and bake the cheesecake for 35–45 minutes, or until the filling has set.

10 Leave the cheesecake to cool in the tin. Push the bottom of the flan tin up to lift out the baked cheesecake. Serve **chilled**, dusted with a little icing sugar.

Black Forest gâteau

This rich chocolate and cherry cake, made with morello cherries, is a speciality of the Black Forest region of south-west Germany. Morello cherries are slightly sour and taste best if they are cooked in a little sugar syrup. You can buy them ready-cooked in jars or cans.

What you need

200g caster sugar
200g butter or margarine
4 eggs
3 tbsp cocoa
150g self raising flour
½ tsp baking powder
425g jar morello cherries, pitted (stones removed)
568ml double cream
75g plain chocolate

What you do

1 **Preheat** the oven to 190°C/375°F/gas mark 5. Cut non-stick baking parchment to fit the bottom of two round 20cm cake tins. Grease the tins and line with parchment.

2 Using an electric whisk, **beat** the sugar and butter or margarine until the mixture is pale and creamy.

3 Beat the eggs and mix half into the butter mixture. Beat in the rest of the egg, a spoonful at a time.

4 Sift the cocoa, flour and baking powder into the mixture and **fold** in – do this by cutting into the mixture with a metal spoon, don't stir.

5 Spoon an equal amount of mixture into each cake tin. Level the surface using the back of a spoon.

6 **Bake** for 20 minutes, or until the cake springs back when pressed. Cool in the tins and then tip the cake out onto a wire cooling rack.

38

7 **Drain** any liquid from the cherries in a sieve. Using an electric whisk, beat the cream until it stands up in peaks. Spread a quarter of it on one sponge, and then scatter over half of the cherries. Place the other sponge on top.

8 Spread the top and sides with cream, keeping some for **piping**.

9 **Grate** the chocolate and, with a palette knife or small spatula, press it onto the sides of the cake.

10 Pipe cream stars around the top of the cake (see page 39) and put the rest of the cherries in the centre. Keep the cake **chilled** and serve the same day.

Raspberries with jelly

Jelly is a favourite food for grown-ups and children in Germany. Fresh raspberries are best for this recipe, but if they are too expensive or out of season you can use **defrosted** frozen raspberries. Loganberries, strawberries and blackberries taste good in this dish, too.

What you need

135g packet
   raspberry jelly
400g fresh raspberries
142ml whipping cream
4 sprigs of mint to
   decorate (optional)

What you do

1 Cut the jelly into cubes and put them in a heatproof measuring jug.

2 Very carefully pour **boiling** water from the kettle into the jug up to the 500ml mark. Stir until the jelly has **dissolved**. Leave to cool for 15 minutes.

3 Divide half the raspberries between four bowls and then pour the jelly over them. Cool the jellies, then put them in the fridge to set for about 3 hours.

4 Arrange the rest of the raspberries equally on the four jellies.

5 Using an electric whisk or hand whisk, beat the cream until just thickened.

6 **Pipe** cream on top of each jelly (see page 39, opposite). If you prefer, put teaspoonfuls of cream on top instead.

7 Decorate each jelly with a sprig of mint and serve straight away.

PIPING CREAM

Fit a star nozzle into a piping bag. Put the bag in a jug and fold the top edges of the piping bag over the sides of the jug. Spoon cream into the piping bag.

Twist the top of the piping bag closed. Hold the twisted part of the bag between your thumb and first finger, with the palm of your hand resting on the bag. Hold the nozzle with your other hand. Squeeze the bag to squirt cream out of the nozzle.

Lebkuchen spicy biscuits

Traditionally, people eat these small, spicy biscuits (pronounced *laybcookhen*) at Christmas in Germany. Monks first baked lebkuchen 700 years ago.

What you need

3 tbsp clear honey
25g caster sugar
1 tbsp vegetable oil
50g dried apricots
25g chopped mixed peel
1 tsp cocoa powder
¾ tsp ground cinnamon
¾ tsp ground cardamom
½ tsp ground cloves
125g plain flour
1½ tsp baking powder
50g ground hazelnuts
25g ground almonds
1 egg yolk

For the icing:
50g plain chocolate
75g icing sugar
pink, green and yellow food
    colouring (optional)
hundreds and thousands

What you do

1 Put the honey, sugar and oil in a small, non-stick saucepan. Warm gently, then stir well. Leave to cool.

2 **Chop** the apricots and mixed peel very finely.

3 **Preheat** the oven to 170°C/325°F/gas mark 3. **Sift** the cocoa, spices, flour and baking powder into a bowl. Add the ground nuts.

4 Add the honey mixture, the chopped fruits and egg yolk to the flour mix. Stir to make a stiff dough.

5 **Knead** the dough into a smooth ball (see page 13). Roll it out until it is about 5mm thick.

6 Cut shapes out of the dough with biscuit cutters, or cut squares or diamonds with a knife. Roll leftovers up again.

7 Place the biscuits on greased baking sheets and **bake** for 12–15 minutes. Lift the biscuits off and leave to cool.

(!) 8 Either break the chocolate into a heatproof bowl and place it over a pan of **simmering** water. Stir from time to time until melted. Or cook the chocolate in the microwave for 1 minute and stir until melted.

9 Lift the bowl out. Using a fork, dip some of the biscuits in the chocolate. Leave to set.

10 Sift the icing sugar. Mix in water, a teaspoonful at a time, to make a stiff icing. If you are using food colouring, divide the icing into three bowls. Add a little colouring to each.

11 Spread or **pipe** icing (see page 39) over the biscuits and sprinkle them with hundreds and thousands. Cool, and store in an airtight tin.

43

Further information

Here are some places to find out more about Germany and German cooking.

Books

Food and Festivals; A Flavour of Germany
Mike Hurst, Hodder Wayland.

Germany and the Germans
Anita Ganeri, Franklin Watts, 2000.

Next Stop, Germany
Fred Martin, Heinemann Library 1998.

Websites

www.globalgourmet.com/destinations/germany/
www.recipesource.com/ethnic/europe/german/

Conversion chart

Ingredients for recipes can be measured in two different ways. Metric measurements use grams and millilitres. Imperial measurements use ounces and fluid ounces. This book uses metric measurements. The chart here shows you how to convert measurements from metric to imperial.

SOLIDS		LIQUIDS	
METRIC	IMPERIAL	METRIC	IMPERIAL
10g	¼ oz	30ml	1 fl oz
15g	½ oz	50ml	2 fl oz
25g	1 oz	75ml	2½ fl oz
50g	1¾ oz	100ml	3½ fl oz
75g	2¾ oz	125ml	4 fl oz
100g	3½ oz	150ml	5 fl oz
150g	5 oz	300ml	10 fl oz
250g	9 oz	600ml	20 fl oz
450g	16 oz	1 litre	30½ fl oz

Healthy eating

This diagram shows you which foods you should eat to stay healthy. Most of your food should come from the bottom of the pyramid. Eat some of the foods from the middle every day. Only eat a little of the foods from the top.

Healthy eating, German style

German food includes plenty of potatoes, bread and dumplings, which belong to the bottom layer. Some Germans like to eat quite a lot of meat, but salads of raw **grated** vegetables are popular and healthy. Germans also enjoy stewed fruits both in sweet and **savoury** dishes, so you can see how healthy German cooking can be.

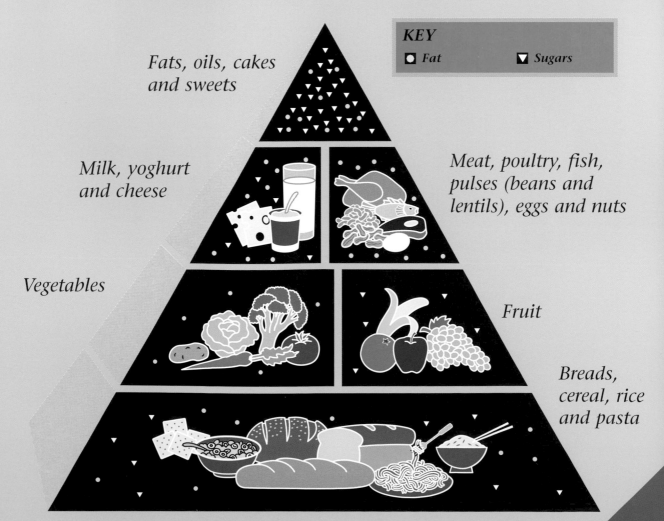

KEY
◻ Fat   ▽ Sugars

Fats, oils, cakes and sweets

Milk, yoghurt and cheese

Meat, poultry, fish, pulses (beans and lentils), eggs and nuts

Vegetables

Fruit

Breads, cereal, rice and pasta

Glossary

bake cook in a hot oven

beat mix something together strongly, such as egg yolks and whites

boiling liquid heated on the hob. Boiling liquid bubbles and steams.

capers seed cases of nasturtium plants which have been pickled or salted

chill put a dish in the fridge for several hours

chop cut something into small pieces using a knife

cover put a lid on a pan or cling wrap over a dish

defrost allow something that is frozen to thaw

dissolve mix something such as sugar until it disappears in a liquid

drain remove liquid, usually by pouring something into a colander or sieve

escalopes thin slices of meat, especially pork or veal

expand when something gets bigger and takes up more space

fermentation process involving bacteria or yeasts to make beer, wine and some preserved foods, like sauerkraut

fertile good for growing things in

fold gently mix in something with a metal spoon using cutting movements

fry cook something in oil in a pan

garnish decorate food, for example, with fresh herbs or tomato slices

grate break something like cheese into very small pieces using a grater

grill cook something under the grill

knead mix ingredients into a smooth dough, such as that for bread. Kneading involves pushing with your hands to make the dough smooth

lard animal fat

marinade sauce that food is left to soak in, so that the food absorbs the flavour of the sauce

nutrients things in food that are good for your body

peel remove the skin of a fruit or vegetable, or the shell of an egg

piping squeezing cream onto a cake in a decorative way

preheat put the oven on so that it is hot when you are ready to use it

rye flour from rye grain is used to make a dark loaf of bread

savoury the opposite of sweet

shred slice into very small, thin pieces

sift push something like flour through a sieve to remove lumps

simmer cook a liquid on the hob. Simmering liquid bubbles and steams gently

slice cut ingredients into thin flat pieces

staple a main ingredient, one found in many dishes

vegetarian food that does not contain any meat or fish. People who don't eat meat are called vegetarians

vines plants that produce grapes

wild boar a type of pig that has dark hairy skin and lives in forests in some countries

Index

Titles in the *World of Recipes* series include:

Hardback   0 431 11714 4

Hardback   0 431 11717 9

Hardback   0 431 11715 2

Hardback   0 431 11716 0

Find out about the other titles in this series on our website www.heinemann.co.uk/library